I'm Reading About

DELAWARE

The First State!

I0886353

GALLOPADE

by Carole Marsh

Copyright ©2014 Carole Marsh/Gallopade
All Rights Reserved.

Printed and Manufactured in Peachtree City, GA., USA
www.gallopade.com

Book design: John Hanson

Editorial manager: Janice Baker

No part of this publication may be reproduced in whole or in part, stored in a retrieval system, or transmitted in any form or by any means, electronic, mechanical, photocopying, recording, or otherwise, without written permission from the publisher.

All companies, product names, or other works mentioned in this book are trademarks of their respective owners, and the names and images used in this book are strictly for editorial purposes; no commercial claims to their use is claimed by the author or publisher.

Delaware is a great state.
It is one of a kind.

What makes Delaware special?
Let's read about it
and see!

NATIVE AMERICANS

Who lived in Delaware first?

Native Americans did!

They moved around to find food.
They hunted in Delaware's woods.
They fished in Delaware's rivers.
They gathered fruits and seeds and nuts.

EXPLORERS

The first explorers came to Delaware in 1609.
They came from the Dutch East India Company.

Henry Hudson was their leader.
He and his men were looking for
a faster route to Asia!

SETTLEMENT

Peter Heyes came from the Netherlands to America.
He started the first settlement in Delaware.
He named it Zwaanendael, which means "Swan Valley."

Delaware was one of the original 13 colonies.

Zwaanendael

STATEHOOD

Delaware was the first state
to join the United States of America!

Isn't it great,
to be a state!
I bet Delaware
could hardly wait!

Delaware became a state in 1787.

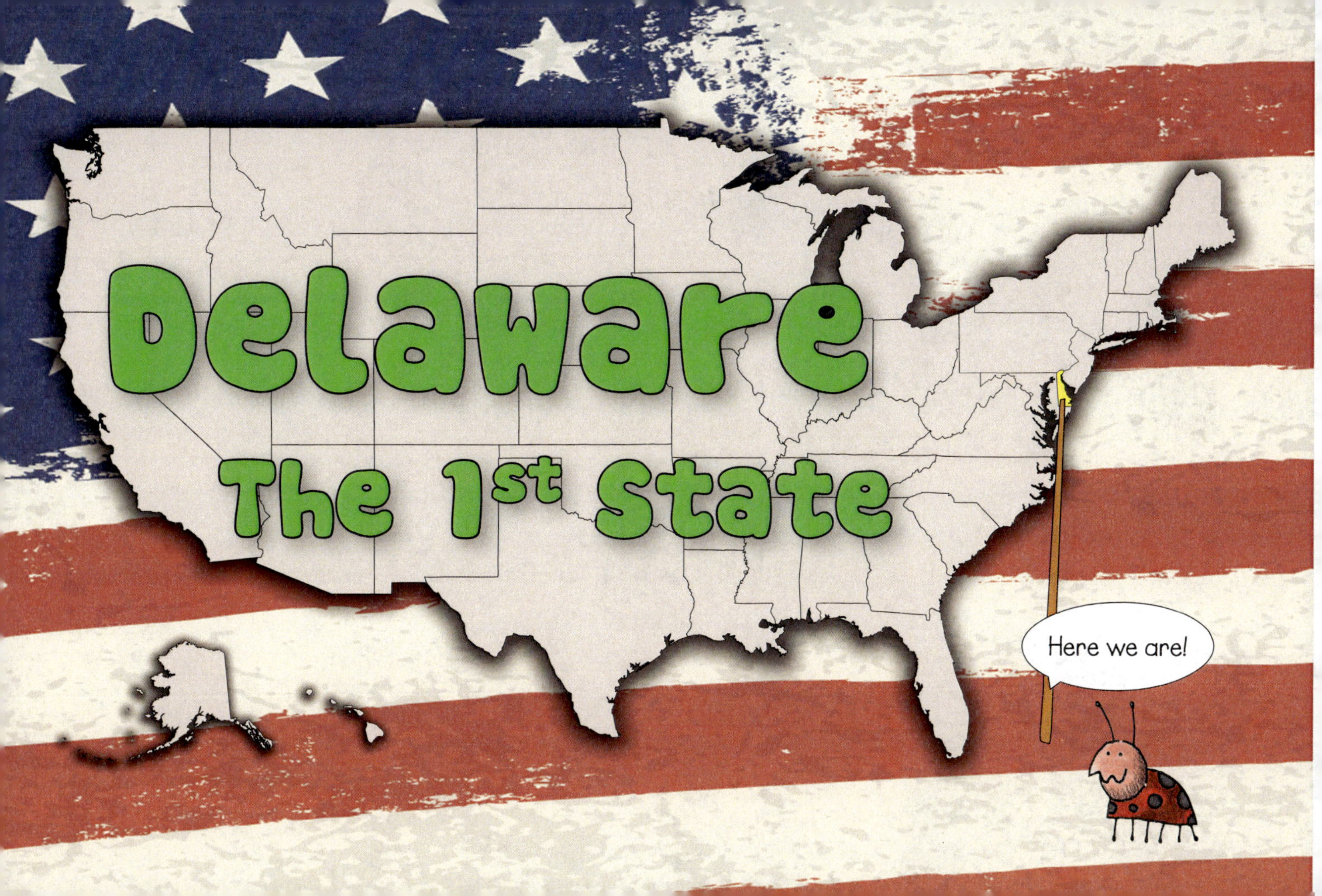
Delaware
The 1st State
Here we are!

FLAG

I am the state flag.
I was adopted in 1913.

What color am I?

Look at me.
What else do you see?

I fly high over the state of Delaware!

LIBERTY AND INDEPENDENCE
DECEMBER 7, 1787

CAPITAL

Say hello to Dover,
the capital city of Delaware!

There is an important building in Dover.
It is the Legislative Hall.
Delaware's laws are made there!

Legislative Hall

SEAL

I am a seal,
but I am not the State Seal.
If I were, I would be very important.
I would be stamped on many official papers.
(Ouch, that might hurt!)

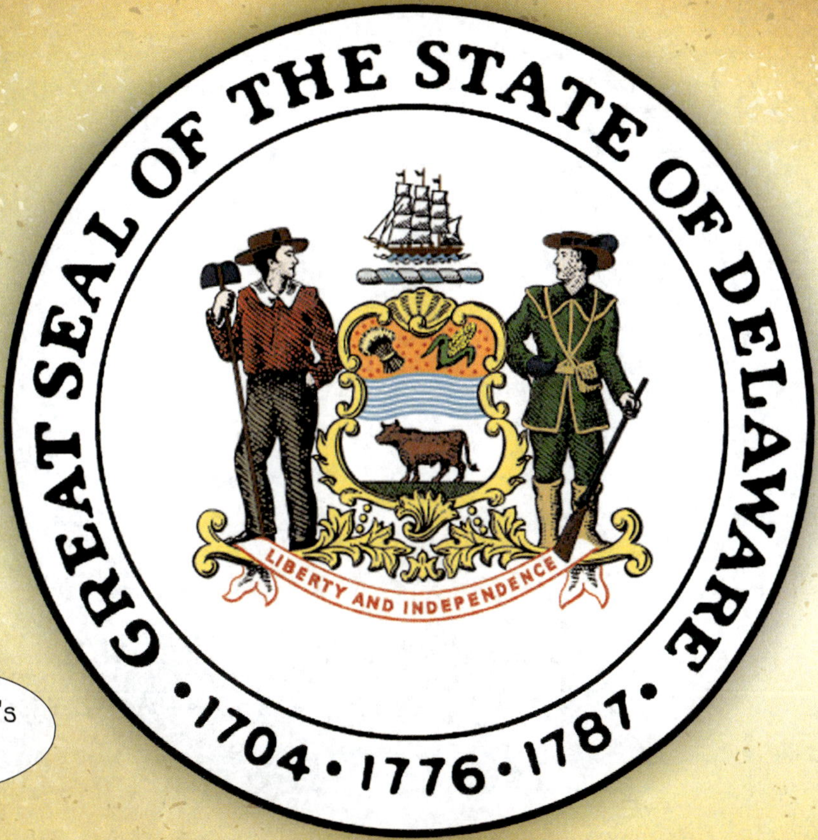
GREAT SEAL OF THE STATE OF DELAWARE
1704 • 1776 • 1787
LIBERTY AND INDEPENDENCE

Now, that's official!

NICKNAME

State nicknames are fun!
State nicknames are great!
They share fun facts
about each state!

Delaware's nickname is "The First State."

Delaware was the first state in
the United States of America!

The First State

BORDERS

Look at Delaware.
Delaware is in a region called "the Northeast."

Delaware borders three other states.
Find them on the map!

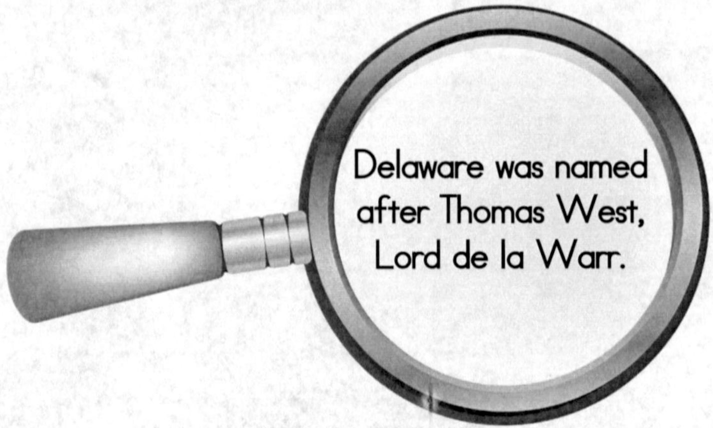

Borders

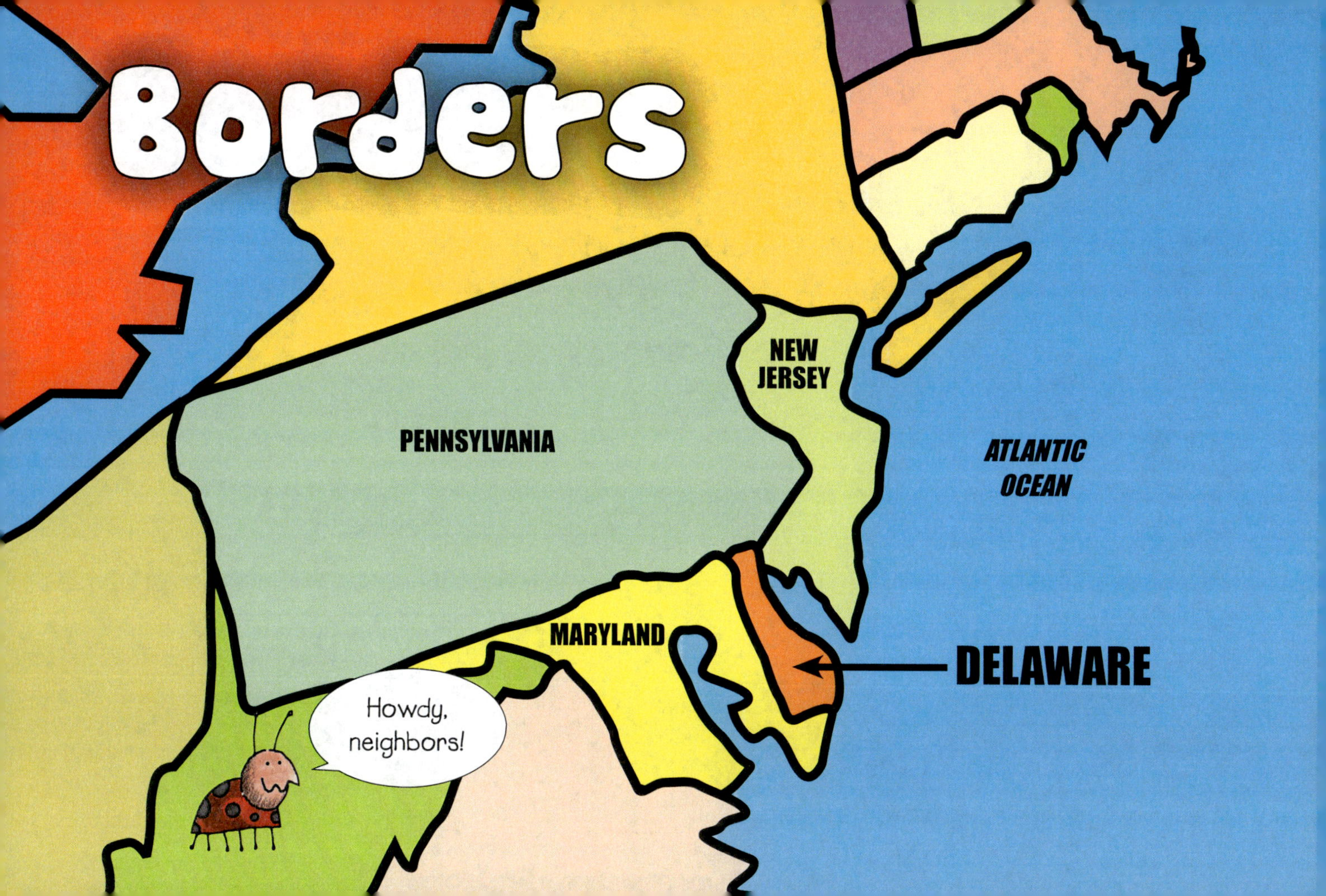
NEW JERSEY
PENNSYLVANIA
ATLANTIC OCEAN
MARYLAND
DELAWARE
Howdy, neighbors!

COUNTIES

Delaware is divided into three counties.
Counties are a form of local government.
Counties provide services that people need!
Those services include:

Schools Parks Libraries Police

Firefighters and More!

Counties

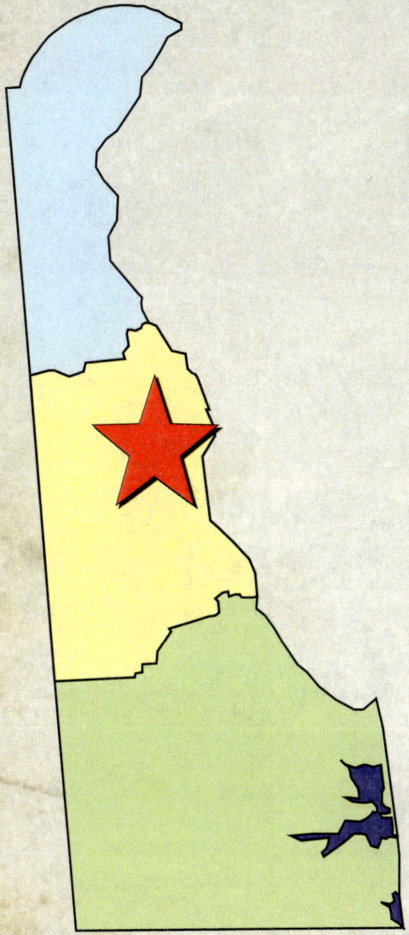

DELAWARE'S CAPITAL, DOVER, IS IN KENT COUNTY.

PEOPLE

Many famous people

Caesar Rodney
Soldier and statesman who signed the Declaration of Independence

E. I. du Pont
Chemist who founded the DuPont chemical company

Thomas MacDonough
Naval officer during the War of 1812

call our state home!

Henry Heimlich
Surgeon who invented the "Heimlich maneuver" to help choking victims

Ruth Ann Minner
First female governor of Delaware

Joseph Biden
U.S. Vice President under President Barack Obama

PEOPLE

Blue Hen

BIRD

I am the state bird, and I strut
and cluck around Delaware farms.

My feathers are fluffy.
They keep me warm.
I flap my wings to tell you "Hello!"

The Delaware state bird is the Blue Hen.

Peach
Blossom

FLOWER

I am the Peach Blossom.
I am the state flower.

I grow where it's warm and sunny.
I bloom in early spring.
I help make Delaware beautiful!

Look at me! Smell me!
I bloom on the peach tree.

American Holly

TREE

I am an American Holly—I'm the state tree.
All over Delaware is where to find me.

My roots run deep, they keep me strong.
My leaves stay green, all year long.

I stand up straight, big and tall.
Don't climb too high—it would hurt to fall!

Ladybug

INSECT

I am the Ladybug
I am the state insect.

I am a type of beetle.
I am red with black polka dots!

Gardeners and farmers love me.
I eat bugs off their plants.
I help Delaware crops grow.

Atlantic Ocean

Let's go to the beach!

We can swim in the waves.
We can play in the sand.

We can build a big castle
where water meets land.

Delaware's beaches are home to many animals:

Sea Turtles **Wild Ponies** **Birds** **Crabs** **Dolphins** **and More!**

BEACHES

Forests

FORESTS

Delaware's forests are the place to be.
Hiking, fishing, camping—
fun for you and me.

Under the shade
of all the tall trees
you can see many beautiful leaves!

Delaware has three state forests—one in each county!

Rivers

RIVERS

Delaware has many rivers.
People like to use rivers for boating and fishing!

This habitat is home to many animals:

Birds Deer Snakes Frogs Fish and More!

The Delaware River forms much of the boundary between Delaware and New Jersey.

Delaware Breakwater East End Light

The Delaware Breakwater East End Light
is a lighthouse.
It is located on the coast of Delaware.

The lighthouse is a tall tower
with a bright light in the top.
The light was used to help guide ships safely home.

Sailors used lighthouses to help
them navigate.

LANDMARK

Delaware Crops

Delaware has many farms.
Why?
Because Delaware has good soil and a mild climate!

Some of the top crops grown in Delaware are:

Corn **Soybeans** **Wheat** **Apples**

Hey!
Don't forget about me!
I am a young chicken.
They call me a "broiler."
Delaware raises lots
of broilers!

AGRICULTURE

Sports in Delaware

SPORTS

Baseball! Basketball! Football!
Delaware has it all.

Whether you like to watch or play,
You are sure to have a ball!

Fightin' Blue Hens

Hornets

& More!

Delaware: The First State

CLAIM TO FAME

Our Founding Fathers wrote the
U.S. Constitution in 1787.

The U.S. Constitution is a set of rules that guide how the government works.
Each of the 13 colonies had to approve it.
Delaware was the first colony to do so!

Delaware approved the U.S. Constitution on December 7, 1787.
That's the day Delaware became the first state!

GLOSSARY

climate: weather conditions in an area over a long period of time

coast: the part of the land near the sea

colony: a settlement ruled by another country

habitat: a place where plants or animals naturally live

laws: rules made by the government

navigate: to plan a route for a ship or other vehicle to take

region: an area that has similar characteristics

settlement: the first community in an area

surgeon: a doctor who treats diseases and injuries by operations